We Love Our Flag

Jean Feldman and Holly Karapetkova

Tune: The Farmer in the Dell

www.rourkeclassroom.com

We love our flag.

We love our flag.

We love America

And we love our flag!

Red, white, and blue

Red, white, and blue

The colors of our country's flag,

Are red, white, and blue!

Fifty stars of white

On a field of blue

Stand for fifty states

Where we live, it's true!

Can You Find Your State?

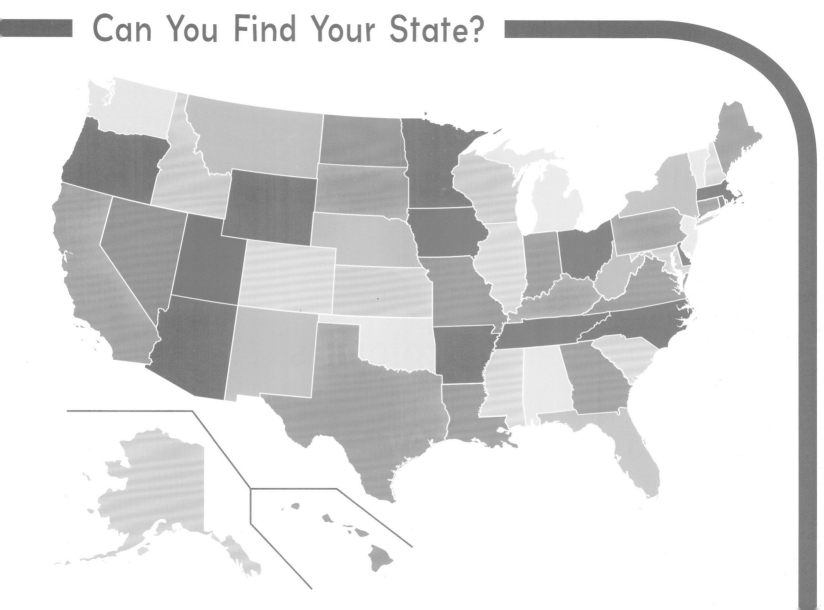

Thirteen stripes

In red and white

Stand for the colonies

For freedom they did fight!

	Colonies
	Territories
	Other countries
	Disputed areas

We love our flag.

We love our flag.

We love America

And we love our flag!

The Pledge of Allegiance

I pledge allegiance to the flag
of the United States of America,
and to the republic for which it stands,
one nation under God, indivisible,
with liberty and justice for all.